SharePoint Apps with LightSwitch

Paul Ferrill

O'REILLY®

Beijing · Cambridge · Farnham · Köln · Sebastopol · Tokyo

SharePoint Apps with LightSwitch

by Paul Ferrill

Published by O'Reilly Media, Inc., 1005 Gravenstein Highway North, Sebastopol, CA 95472.

O'Reilly books may be purchased for educational, business, or sales promotional use. Online editions are also available for most titles (*http://my.safaribooksonline.com*). For more information, contact our corporate/institutional sales department: 800-998-9938 or *corporate@oreilly.com*.

Editor: Rachel Roumeliotis		**Cover Designer:** Karen Montgomery	
Production Editor: Holly Bauer		**Interior Designer:** David Futato	
Proofreader: Holly Bauer		**Illustrator:** Robert Romano	

Revision History for the First Edition:

2012-03-30   First release

See *http://oreilly.com/catalog/errata.csp?isbn=9781449321161* for release details.

ISBN: 978-1-449-32116-1

[LSI]

1333040657

Table of Contents

Preface

This book is about developing SharePoint applications using Microsoft's Visual Studio LightSwitch product. The overall goal of this book is to present enough information by way of worked examples to help you get started writing SharePoint applications using Visual Studio LightSwitch.

Microsoft offers Visual Studio LightSwitch as both a stand-alone product and as an add-on to the full version of Visual Studio. Most of the sample applications presented in this book can be completed using the basic version, with just a few exceptions. Any work involving the building of LightSwitch extensions requires the full version of Visual Studio. Building Silverlight controls is another case where you'll need the full version. Microsoft does offer a trial version of Visual Studio 2010 Ultimate if you just want to check it out.

Audience

While it would probably suffice to say this book is for any person interested in the Visual Studio LightSwitch product by itself, the focus is on building applications specifically targeted at SharePoint. Programming experience isn't necessary, but I will look at writing code to add functionality to some of the examples. It's entirely possible to build fully functional Visual Studio LightSwitch applications without writing a single line of code if that's what you're looking for.

Experienced programmers who are looking for a way to quickly and efficiently build stand-alone applications to interact with a SharePoint site should benefit from the book as well. The programming model is completely different from the typical SharePoint development cycle, so expect to see some new material. There are, however, enough similarities to building typical Windows Forms apps that you should be able to pick it up quickly enough.

Contents of This Book

Chapter 1, *Introduction*, introduces you to the product itself and discusses some of the concepts used in developing stand-alone applications. The good news is you can use the same code to build web applications as well. I'll also discuss some of the key pieces of SharePoint, since that's the main target.

Chapter 2, *Getting Started*, covers the installation of both Visual Studio LightSwitch and SharePoint.

Chapter 3, *Simple Applications*, shows you how to build simple applications requiring no coding.

Chapter 4, *Power User Applications*, moves into slightly more complex samples with some code to perform specific functions.

Chapter 5, *Application Integration*, details the integration of LightSwitch applications with other data sources like CSV files, importing and exporting to Excel, a SQLite database, and Google data.

Conventions Used in This Book

The following typographical conventions are used in this book:

Italic
> Indicates new terms, URLs, email addresses, filenames, and file extensions.

`Constant width`
> Used for program listings, as well as within paragraphs to refer to program elements such as variable or function names, databases, data types, environment variables, statements, and keywords.

`Constant width bold`
> Shows commands or other text that should be typed literally by the user.

`Constant width italic`
> Shows text that should be replaced with user-supplied values or by values determined by context.

This icon signifies a tip, suggestion, or general note.

This icon indicates a warning or caution.

Using Code Examples

This book is here to help you get your job done. In general, you may use the code in this book in your programs and documentation. You do not need to contact us for permission unless you're reproducing a significant portion of the code. For example, writing a program that uses several chunks of code from this book does not require permission. Selling or distributing a CD-ROM of examples from O'Reilly books does require permission. Answering a question by citing this book and quoting example code does not require permission. Incorporating a significant amount of example code from this book into your product's documentation does require permission.

We appreciate, but do not require, attribution. An attribution usually includes the title, author, publisher, and ISBN. For example: "*SharePoint Apps with LightSwitch* by Paul Ferrill (O'Reilly). Copyright 2012 Paul Ferrill, 978-1-449-32116-1."

If you feel your use of code examples falls outside fair use or the permission given above, feel free to contact us at *permissions@oreilly.com*.

Safari® Books Online

 Safari Books Online (*www.safaribooksonline.com*) is an on-demand digital library that delivers expert content in both book and video form from the world's leading authors in technology and business.

Technology professionals, software developers, web designers, and business and creative professionals use Safari Books Online as their primary resource for research, problem solving, learning, and certification training.

Safari Books Online offers a range of product mixes and pricing programs for organizations, government agencies, and individuals. Subscribers have access to thousands of books, training videos, and prepublication manuscripts in one fully searchable database from publishers like O'Reilly Media, Prentice Hall Professional, Addison-Wesley Professional, Microsoft Press, Sams, Que, Peachpit Press, Focal Press, Cisco Press, John Wiley & Sons, Syngress, Morgan Kaufmann, IBM Redbooks, Packt, Adobe Press, FT Press, Apress, Manning, New Riders, McGraw-Hill, Jones & Bartlett, Course Technology, and dozens more. For more information about Safari Books Online, please visit us online.

How to Contact Us

Please address comments and questions concerning this book to the publisher:

O'Reilly Media, Inc.
1005 Gravenstein Highway North
Sebastopol, CA 95472
800-998-9938 (in the United States or Canada)
707-829-0515 (international or local)
707-829-0104 (fax)

We have a web page for this book, where we list errata, examples, and any additional information. You can access this page at:

http://oreil.ly/sharepoint-apps-lightswitch

To comment or ask technical questions about this book, send email to:

bookquestions@oreilly.com

For more information about our books, courses, conferences, and news, see our website at *http://www.oreilly.com*.

Find us on Facebook: *http://facebook.com/oreilly*

Follow us on Twitter: *http://twitter.com/oreillymedia*

Watch us on YouTube: *http://www.youtube.com/oreillymedia*

Acknowledgments

Thanks to my wife, Sandy, for her help and support. You truly are the love of my life. Additional thanks to my children for putting up with an absent daddy. I'd like to thank Carmen Taglienti for his technical review. Special thanks to Rachel Roumeliotis for the opportunity to bring this project to life.

Introduction

The important thing to point out right from the start is that Visual Studio LightSwitch in its stand-alone version shares much of the same functionality as the full version of Visual Studio. Figure 1-1 shows the opening screen of Visual Studio LightSwitch, which looks just like what you would see if you launched the full version. There are differences, however, in many ways. Visual Studio LightSwitch uses a model-based approach to building applications and a declarative method of creating screens. That means you won't have the familiar drag-and-drop design surface for your screens you'd expect with a typical C# or VB.NET Windows application.

Many of the same menus, like the Server Explorer, are still available but are hidden by default. Other menus, like the toolbox with various screen elements, are not there in the stand-alone version. You will be able to debug your applications by using the normal process of setting breakpoints, examining variables, and single-stepping through your code. The only hitch here is you have to write code to actually debug it. In some cases, it's helpful to put in a debug line in a routine you know will run just to poke around and see what variables are used.

If you do start poking around underneath the covers of the Microsoft code created for every LightSwitch app, you'll quickly find out that there's a lot of code there. It's probably best that you not change any of the automatically generated code unless you want to break something. There are plenty of places to add your own custom changes without modifying the default code. You'll see this a little later on when I introduce you to the different designers.

Basic Concepts and Terms

Visual Studio LightSwitch uses the classic three-tier architecture approach to building applications consisting of Presentation, Logic, and Storage. If you look under the covers of the Presentation level, you'll find Silverlight 4.0 as the underlying technology. This is what makes it possible to target your applications at both the desktop and a web

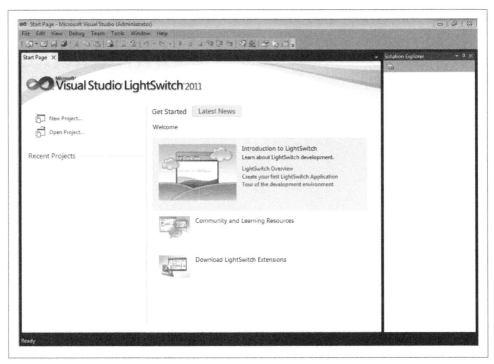

Figure 1-1. Initial LightSwitch screen

browser. It also limits you somewhat to building your user interface (UI) on top of the Silverlight toolkit.

The Logic tier utilizes Windows Communication Foundation (WCF) Rich Internet Application (RIA) Services on top of ASP.NET 4.0. These services can be hosted locally on a client machine, on a server running IIS 7, or in the cloud via a Windows Azure Web Role. Primary Storage utilizes Microsoft SQL Server or SQL Azure. Stand-alone apps require Microsoft SQL Server Express 2008.

Visual Studio LightSwitch borrows a great deal from the Entity Framework for its data model. All LightSwitch data services use an Entity Framework ObjectContext as the primary way of communicating with the data tier. All LightSwitch applications also use the Model, View, View-Model (MVVM) pattern. MVVM is a Windows Presentation Foundation (WPF) design pattern that has gained a significant following since its introduction. The key rationale for MVVM is the separation of functionality between the View, or UI code; the code underneath or behind the View (View-Model); and the code that interfaces to the data or model.

What Is Visual Studio LightSwitch?

Visual Studio LightSwitch is a tool for building business applications using either C# or VB.NET. Having said that, it's entirely possible to build a functional application using Visual Studio LightSwitch without actually writing a single line of code. The flow of building an application using Visual Studio LightSwitch starts with identifying data sources either from scratch or from an existing source. If you're creating a new database from scratch, you'll be using Microsoft SQL Server Express as the storage and retrieval engine. The other out-of-the-box supported data source is Microsoft SharePoint. I'll talk about that more in a bit.

The Visual Studio LightSwitch application uses a number of different windows to present information pertinent to the current activity. Some windows, such as the Solution Explorer and Properties page (see Figure 1-2), are visible all the time unless closed. Microsoft calls this a pinned window, meaning it is pinned to the visible surface of the application.

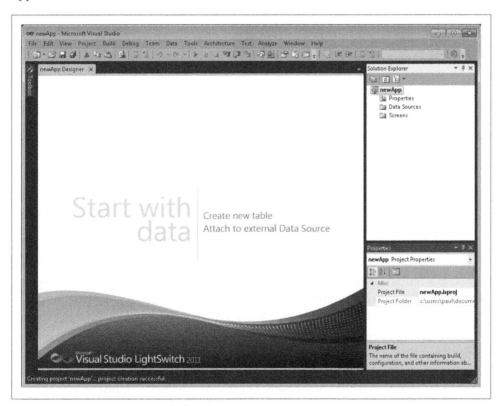

Figure 1-2. First screen presented after choosing New Project

Visual Studio LightSwitch uses the concept of a designer to simplify the process of building applications. The Data Designer is used to create or modify the structure of a data table (see Figure 1-3). The toolbar across the top of the designer gives the user quick access to functions related to the current activity. In the case of the Data Designer, this includes the ability to add a Relationship, Computed Property, Query, Screen or New Table. The other designers have a similar toolbar with different functions.

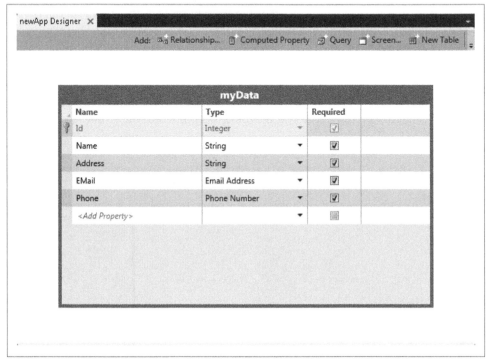

Figure 1-3. The Table Designer is for specifying data structure

Building queries to select and sort data is another key aspect of building applications with Visual Studio LightSwitch. The Query Designer functions in much the same way as the Table Designer, giving you the ability to create a query against any defined data source. Figure 1-4 shows a parameterized query against the Name field.

Clicking the Add Screen button on the Designer toolbar will launch the Screen Designer. You can also switch to the Screen Designer from the Solution Explorer by either right-clicking on the Screen folder and choosing Add Screen or by double-clicking on any existing screen. Screens are linked to either a data source or a query.

If you have used Visual Studio in the past to create Windows Forms applications, you may find the declarative nature of building screens with Visual Studio LightSwitch a little cumbersome at first. The Screen Designer generates the user interface elements automatically and provides much more control over the layout of information without

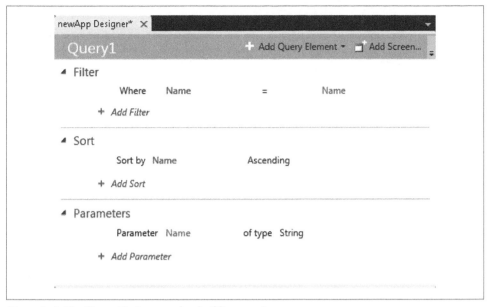

Figure 1-4. The Query Designer makes building queries a snap

having to manually drag and drop each item from the toolbar. This makes building simple data information screens really fast.

Figure 1-5 shows what you will see for a typical screen with the tree view of controls and data items on the right and the source data entities and screen methods on the left. There are convenience items, such as the Edit Query link, available to quickly take you to another task.

You do have the ability to write code in situations where you need more functionality. All designers have a button or link labeled Write Code (see Figure 1-5). It might be hidden because of the window size, but it will appear if you click on the little downward-pointing arrow on the rightmost end of the designer toolbar (see Figures 1-3 and 1-4). If you click on the Write Code link, you'll be presented with a list of available methods applicable to the current screen (see Figure 1-6).

The methods should be recognizable if you've written any code using Visual Studio before. In this example, the current screen is named EditablemyDatasGrid and has a number of general methods associated with it. The `_Activated` method runs just after the screen is activated while the `_Closing` method runs just before the screen closes.

If you click on one of the methods, it will open the Visual Studio code editor inside that method (see Figure 1-7). Now you have the full capabilities of writing code, such as auto completion, code formatting, and IntelliSense.

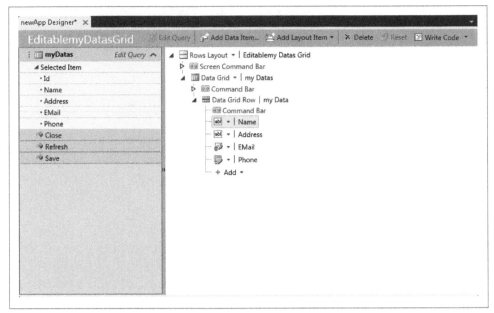

Figure 1-5. The Screen Designer shows a tree view of all elements

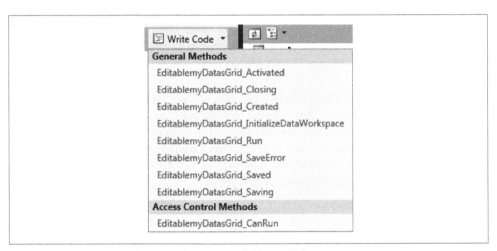

Figure 1-6. The Write Code button displays available methods

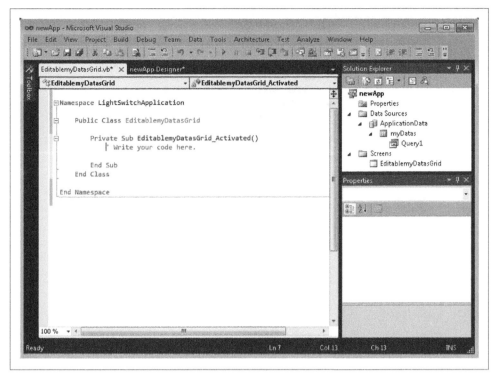

Figure 1-7. Visual Studio code editor

The last thing I want to point out about the Visual Studio LightSwitch application is the two different modes of the Solution Explorer. By default, the Solution Explorer displays items in a Logical View where the information mimics the different functional parts of a LightSwitch application. In general, this consists of Data Sources and Screens. You can view a solution in a more traditional Visual Studio fashion by clicking on the Project View dropdown button (fourth button from the left under Solution Explorer in Figure 1-7).

This will give you the option to switch to File View. Figure 1-8 shows what you would see for our demo app.

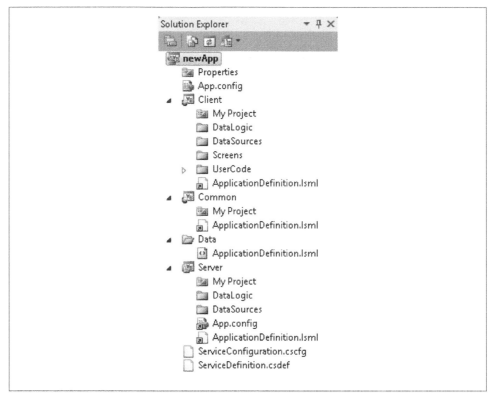

Figure 1-8. Solution Explorer in File View mode

I'll show you when this mode is needed in a later chapter.

SharePoint Basics

Visual Studio LightSwitch requires SharePoint 2010 or higher, primarily because of OData support. All communication between a LightSwitch app and SharePoint uses a list. Whenever you add an external data source to your LightSwitch application and choose SharePoint, you'll be presented with a dialog containing all available Lists on the site. Figure 1-9 shows an example of the lists you will find on a typical SharePoint site.

There is one list automatically selected by default, named UserInformationList. This list contains information about all users known to the SharePoint site. It is selected by default since virtually every other list links to it in some way. Access to any list is controlled by SharePoint permissions. You will need to have site administrator privileges if you want to modify the UserInformationList. Not having the appropriate permissions will result in read-only fields when Visual Studio LightSwitch creates a screen from the

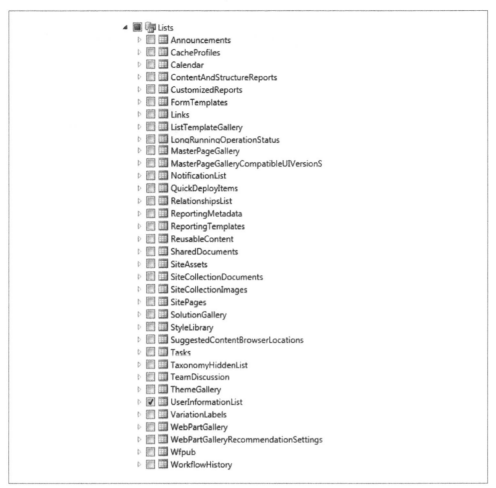

Figure 1-9. List of available SharePoint Lists

SharePoint list. In some cases, this could be the behavior you want if you simply need to present information to the user without allowing any changes to be made.

Visual Studio LightSwitch allows you to change the way incoming SharePoint fields are displayed to the user. A good example of this is the Task list. By default, all date fields have both date and time associated with them. You can change this to display only the date in the Data Designer.

All the SharePoint examples in this book are based on a demo site made available by Microsoft for a fictional company named Contoso. Figure 1-10 shows the home screen for the URL *http://intranet.contoso.com*. It's based on a stock SharePoint 2010 installation and includes a minimal set of content. We'll be adding to the Calendar and Tasks list for several of the sample applications.

Figure 1-10. Main SharePoint demo page

The SharePoint Tasks list will be the focus of several examples in the following chapters. Figure 1-11 shows this list from within SharePoint with Task 1 through Task 9 assigned to me.

		Type	Title	Assigned To	Status	Priority	Due Date	% Complete	Predecessors	Related Content
			Create Project Plan	David Bossard	Not Started	(2) Normal				
			Build Presentation Slides	David Bossard	Not Started	(2) Normal				
			Build Excel Budget Spreadsheet	David Bossard	Not Started	(2) Normal				
			Task1	Paul Ferrill	Not Started	(2) Normal		90 %		
			Task 2	Paul Ferrill	Not Started	(2) Normal		80 %		
			Task 3	Paul Ferrill	Not Started	(2) Normal		70 %		
			Task 4	Paul Ferrill	Not Started	(2) Normal		60 %		
			Task 5	Paul Ferrill	Not Started	(2) Normal		50 %		
			Task 6	Paul Ferrill	Not Started	(2) Normal		40 %		
			Task 7	Paul Ferrill	Not Started	(2) Normal		30 %		
			Task 8	Paul Ferrill	Not Started	(2) Normal		20 %		
			Task 9	Paul Ferrill	In Progress	(2) Normal		10 %		

Figure 1-11. SharePoint tasks are the main connecting point

Summary

In this chapter, I introduced you to Visual Studio LightSwitch and many of the concepts you will see demonstrated in the rest of the book. It's important to understand the architecture behind LightSwitch applications if you want to go beyond the basics of building without code. Knowing where to add your customization is more than half the battle.

Since the focus of the book is on building SharePoint applications, it's also important to understand the basic mechanism of communication to and from a SharePoint site. All interaction from the perspective of permissions is controlled by SharePoint, so you'll either need to know how to make administrative changes to individual users yourself or know the person able to make them for you.

You'll want to set up a separate test server or machine to try out the code in this book. I'll walk you through getting that set up in Chapter 2.

Getting Started

One of the things you're going to need if you want to do SharePoint development is a SharePoint server. If you already have access to a SharePoint server, you're all set. In case you don't, I'll walk you through the process of getting one set up and configured. There are a few other options as well, including downloading a ready-made virtual machine from Microsoft. The only downside there is you'll need a fairly hefty system running Windows Server 2008 R2 Enterprise with the Hyper-V role installed. I used a computer based on an AMD 6-Core CPU with 16 GB of memory and it performed well. Memory is probably the most important thing when it comes to running multiple VMs, so the more, the better.

Other options include installing SharePoint on a Windows 7 client machine. This might be appealing to an individual developer looking to get familiar with SharePoint and the tools for developing applications. I'll take a quick look at that option and give you enough information to try it out should you so choose. For the examples in this book, I'll use the Microsoft VHD, as it comes preconfigured with everything needed including sample data.

Virtual Environment Setup

If you decide to go the Windows Server and virtual machine route versus physical, you'll need a system with at least 16 GB of memory and a CPU capable of supporting native virtualization. In some cases, you will need to enable that feature in the BIOS of the system. For the purposes of the examples in this book, I'm using a self-built server based on an Asus M4A89GTD Pro motherboard with 16 GB of memory and an AMD 1090T 6-core CPU. For the operating system, I installed Windows Server 2008 R2 SP1 Enterprise Edition.

Once you have Windows Server installed, you must install the Hyper-V role in order to run multiple virtual machines. Microsoft has made available a packaged download of SharePoint trial virtual machines (VMs), which includes SharePoint 2010, Office

2010, and Project Server 2010. As this writing, you can find it at *http://www.microsoft .com/download/en/details.aspx?displaylang=en&id=27417*.

It's titled "2010 Information Worker Demonstration and Evaluation Virtual Machine (SP1)." You will want to get the Microsoft Word document from the same location with instructions on how to set up and configure your host machine to run the VMs. The first VM is the one you will want to get for working through the examples in this book.

You can either click on each of the 23 download links or use a little trick that I prefer: basically, you right-click on one of the download links and copy the URL to the clipboard. Then, open up Notepad and paste the link there. You'll need a copy of the open source wget (*http://sourceforge.net/projects/gnuwin32/files/wget/1.11.4-1/wget-1.11.4 -1-setup.exe/download*) program for this trick to work. I used wget64 since my main workstation runs the 64-bit version of Windows 7. Finally, you copy/paste the source URL enough times to download each of the files and then edit the name to get the correct file. Here's what the first four lines of my *wget.bat* file look like:

```
wget64 http://download.microsoft.com/download/6/B/6/6B63BAC2-8CCF-4A45-9E4E-
AA3BE0E735C7/2010-10a.part01.exe
wget64 http://download.microsoft.com/download/6/B/6/6B63BAC2-8CCF-4A45-9E4E-
AA3BE0E735C7/2010-10a.part02.rar
wget64 http://download.microsoft.com/download/6/B/6/6B63BAC2-8CCF-4A45-9E4E-
AA3BE0E735C7/2010-10a.part03.rar
wget64 http://download.microsoft.com/download/6/B/6/6B63BAC2-8CCF-4A45-9E4E-
AA3BE0E735C7/2010-10a.part04.rar
```

Notice that the first file has an extension of *.exe*, and the others end with *.rar*. That's because Microsoft used the RAR archive tool to create a multipart archive in order to split up the huge download size into smaller chunks. When the download finishes, you have to run the first file, *2010-10a.part01.exe*, to put the chunks back together. It will look something like Figure 2-1.

When this is complete, you should see a directory like the one in Figure 2-2.

There are a few things that need to be accomplished before we can use this VM. First, we need to run the Hyper-V network manager tool and define an "Internal" network for use by the demo machine. This, in effect, creates a virtual switch through which all VMs may connect. Bring up this screen by selecting it from the "Actions" menu with the server selected under Hyper-V role in Server Manager (see Figure 2-3).

Figure 2-4 shows the Virtual Network Manager screen with the Internal network high-lighted. Clicking the Add button presents one more dialog screen where you specify the name of the new network. For our purposes, we'll use Internal. Once the Internal network is created, it will show up in the list of network adapters on the host machine. We need to change the IP address of this network to match that of the VM. The quickest way to do that is to right-click on the network icon in the system tray and choose "Open Network and Sharing Center." From there, choose "Change Adapter Settings."

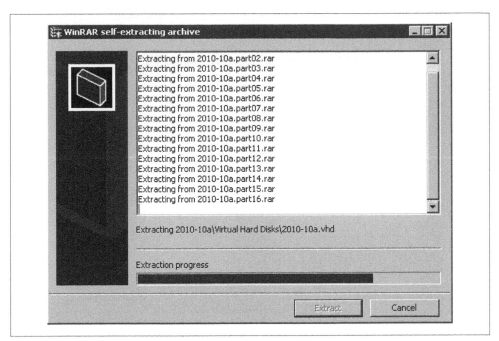

Figure 2-1. *Reassembling the downloaded pieces*

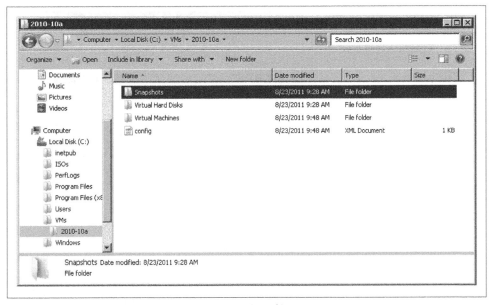

Figure 2-2. *Directory with SharePoint virtual machine files*

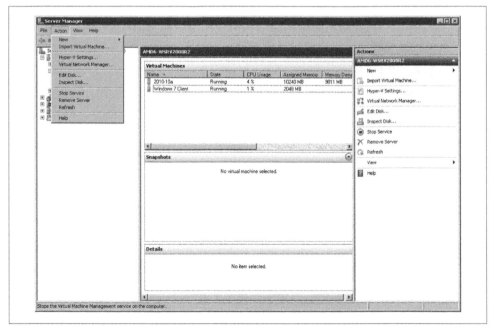

Figure 2-3. Server Manager with Hyper-V Manager selected

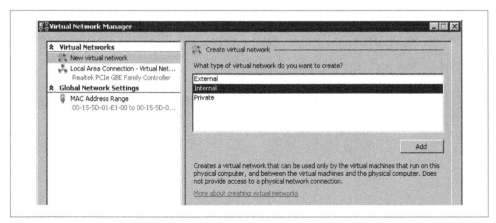

Figure 2-4. Virtual Network Manager screen

To change the IP address, right-click on the Internal network device and choose Properties. Then highlight "Internet Protocol Version 4 (TCP/IPv4)" and click the Properties button. Next, select the "Use the following IP address:" radio button and enter the address 192.168.150.6. The "Use the following DNS server addresses" radio button will automatically be checked from the last step, allowing you to enter the address of 192.168.150.1 (see Figure 2-5). Once that's complete, click OK and close the other network properties windows.

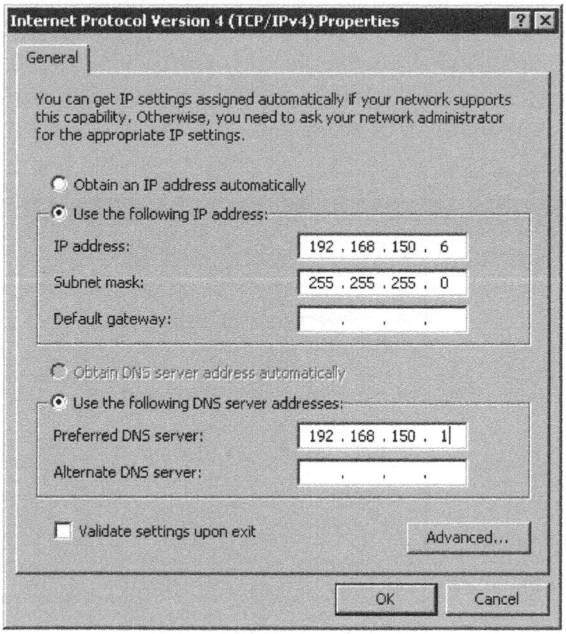

Figure 2-5. Assigning the network switch an IP address

Now that we have all the plumbing in place, it's time to get the main VM configured. This is a relatively simple process, as you just import the downloaded machine. Notice in Figure 2-6 that you must choose the top-level directory where you unpacked the downloaded files.

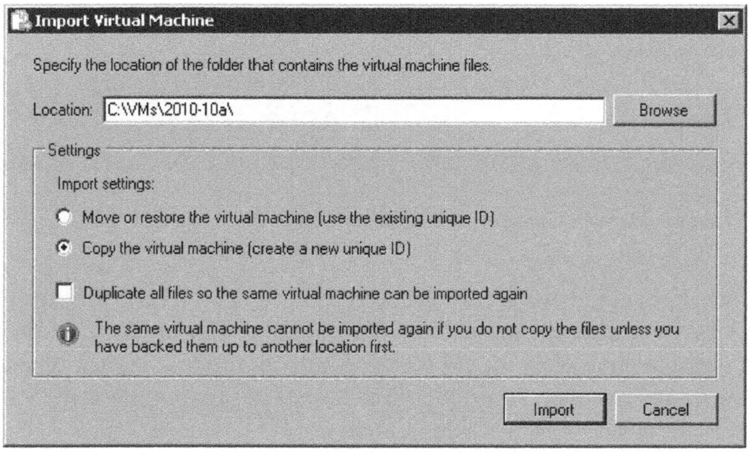

Figure 2-6. Import Virtual Machine dialog

There are a few things that need adjusting before we actually launch the server. Since we're using Windows Server 2008 R2 SP1, we have the ability to use the Dynamic Memory option. Figure 2-7 shows how to configure this. The 10240 MB max memory number is the highest you want to go if you also use a client VM with 2 GB of memory as we did. This gives about 2 GB of headroom on a 16 GB server.

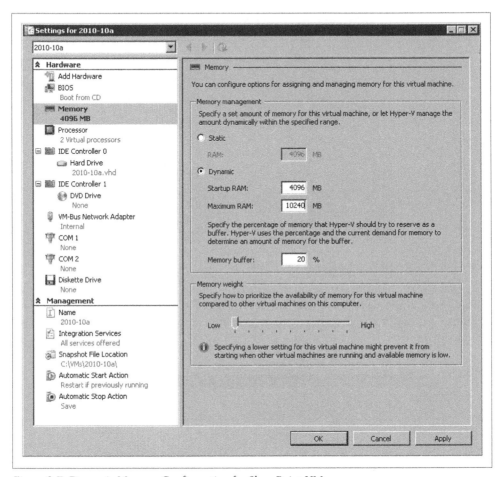

Figure 2-7. Dynamic Memory Configuration for SharePoint VM

With these changes made, we're ready to start the VM. You'll probably need to restart the VM at least once after the initial boot. The default password for the administrator account is pass@word1. You should see a command window launch when you first log in to "warm-up" the SharePoint site. This consists of programmatically visiting each of the SharePoint pages to cache them in memory.

You should be able to launch Internet Explorer and see the default SharePoint screen for intranet.contoso.com. The SharePoint Central Administration page is available from the Windows Start menu. If everything is working correctly, you should see a screen like the one in Figure 2-8.

There are a number of good blog posts with instructions on how to get SharePoint configured in a virtual machine. A quick Google search for "sharepoint vm it worker" will return a number of good resources to help get you going. Microsoft's Channel 9 website (*http://channel9.msdn.com/*) also has a number of video presentations on using the fictional Contoso Company virtual machine. Just enter "SharePoint IT worker VM" in the search box on the home page and you'll get a list of all related content.

I should also mention at this point the option of installing SharePoint on a Windows 7 machine. I got this working on a Dell XPS M1330 laptop, which has 6 GB of memory and a 2.4 GHz Intel Core 2 Duo processor. It wasn't as fast as the server-based option, but it worked well for times when I was traveling and wanted to work on some of the code for the book. If you do a Google search for "SharePoint on Windows 7," you'll find several methods for getting this working, including a script to automate the process (*http://gallery.technet.microsoft.com/scriptcenter/a88cad83-f595-4487-940e -f678ce47eb5f*).

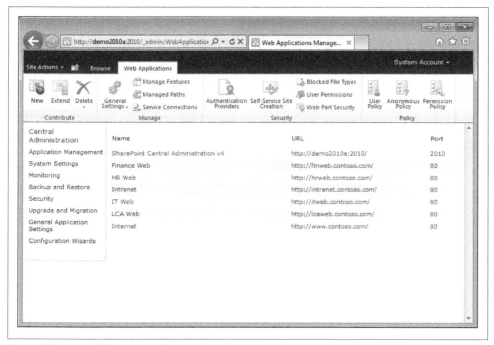

Figure 2-8. Demo SharePoint administration page

The VMs require activation, which means you must connect to the Internet. In order to activate Windows, you must add a second network card to each VM in Hyper-V and connect it to the external network. Once connected, you can activate Windows Server within the Virtual Machine, and the VM will run for 180 days.

Visual Studio LightSwitch Install

There are two basic options available for installing Visual Studio LightSwitch. If you already have Visual Studio Professional 2010, you can install LightSwitch as an add-in. If not, you have the option of installing Visual Studio LightSwitch as a stand-alone tool. Microsoft offers a 90-day trial version of LightSwitch, which you can download from their download center. Be aware that the trial actually lasts for 30 days, and you can register for an additional 60 days.

The main SharePoint VM mentioned earlier comes with Visual Studio 2010 Professional installed. It does have SP1 installed, which is a prerequisite for installing Visual Studio LightSwitch. As of this writing, there is one additional action that must be taken before running the Visual Studio LightSwitch install program. One of the steps accomplished by the installation process is to install SQL Server Express 2008. This step will fail as a part of the LightSwitch installer when executed on the SharePoint VM. It is possible to download the SQL Server Express 2008 installer and run it separately (*http: //msdn.microsoft.com/en-us/evalcenter/ff978728.aspx?wt.mc_id=MEC_36_1_5*). SQL Server Express 2008 is required by Visual Studio LightSwitch, so you must successfully install it before moving on.

Two things are required to make this work. First, you have to run the SQL Server Express 2008 setup program with administrator privileges. The easiest way to do this is to simply right-click on the install file from Windows Explorer and select "Run as administrator" (see Figure 2-9). Second, you must wade through the SQL Express installer screens.

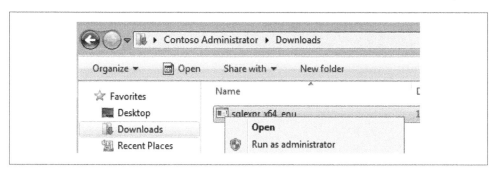

Figure 2-9. Run SQL Express Setup as Administrator

When you launch the setup program, you should see a screen like the one shown in Figure 2-10. Select Installation from the lefthand pane and then chose to install a new SQL instance by selecting "New SQL Server stand-alone installation or add features to an existing installation." This will launch a process that will check to make sure you have all the prerequisites needed to install the new instance. Clicking OK on this screen will take you to another screen labeled Setup Support Files. Clicking Install will launch another process to check to make sure the system is configured properly.

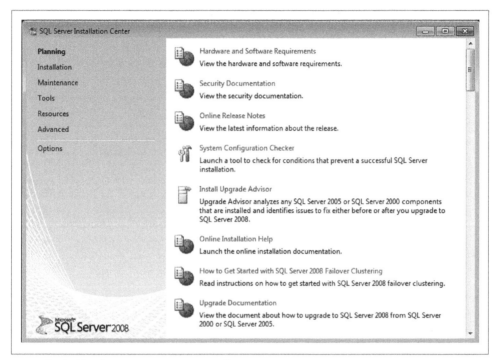

Figure 2-10. SQL Server Express 2008 installation screen

At this point, you should see a screen entitled Installation Type with "Perform a new installation of SQL Server 2008" selected by default and a list of all existing instances. Clicking Next will then take you to a screen for entering a product key, which is not necessary for SQL Express, so just click Next here. Now you must check the box next to "I accept the license terms" to accept Microsoft's license agreement for SQL Server 2008 Express Edition.

Stay with me here—there are just a few more screens. On the Feature Selection page, check the Database Engine Services box and click Next. Finally, we come to the page where you must make sure the "Named instance" box contains SQLExpress (see Figure 2-11). It typically uses this by default unless there is another instance already installed with that name.

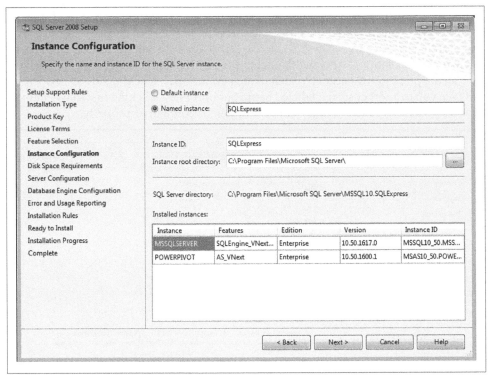

Figure 2-11. SQL Server Express 2008 Setup

Clicking Next here takes you to the Disk Space Requirements screen. It will check to see if you have enough room on the device where you're trying to install SQL Server Express 2008. From here, you'll be taken to the Server Configuration screen by clicking Next. You must select an account name for the SQL Server database engine as shown in Figure 2-12.

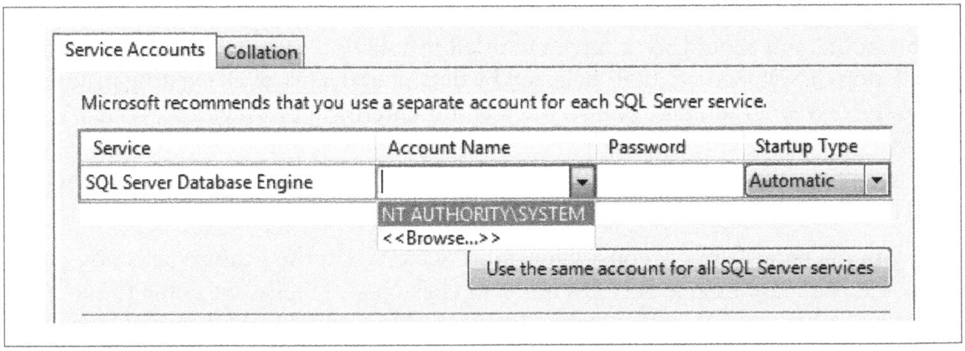

Figure 2-12. SQL Server Database Service Account

On the next screen, click Add Current User and then Next. The next screen allows you to opt in or out of sending information to Microsoft. One final check is made and results presented on the next screen, giving you one more chance to cancel should you desire. Clicking Next will launch the installation process. Once that completes, you should be able to run the Visual Studio LightSwitch installer on the SharePoint VM without issue.

For the stand-alone option, you'll need at least 3 GB of disk space available to install Visual Studio LightSwitch. The initial download is quite small, as it will download all necessary components over the Web. Figure 2-13 shows what you should see as the download process progresses.

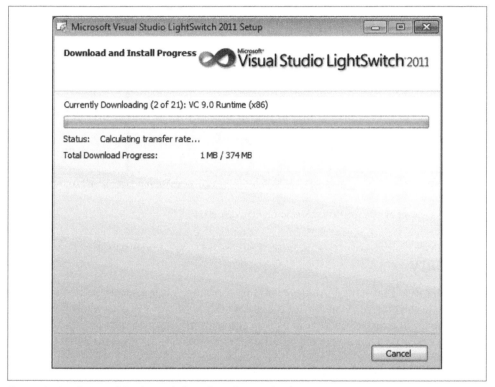

Figure 2-13. TheVisual Studio LightSwitch Web Download Process

You can install Visual Studio LightSwitch on any client workstation with 1 GB of memory and at least a 1.6 GHz CPU running Windows XP with SP3, Windows Vista (32- or 64-bit) with SP2, or Windows 7 (32- or 64-bit). If you choose to install using a virtual machine, you'll need to allocate at least 1.5 GB of memory. Whatever operating system you use, you'll need to join the workstation (or VM) to the Contoso.com domain to avoid any account privilege issues. When the installation process completes, you should be able to launch Visual Studio LightSwitch 2011 and see a screen like the one shown in Figure 2-14.

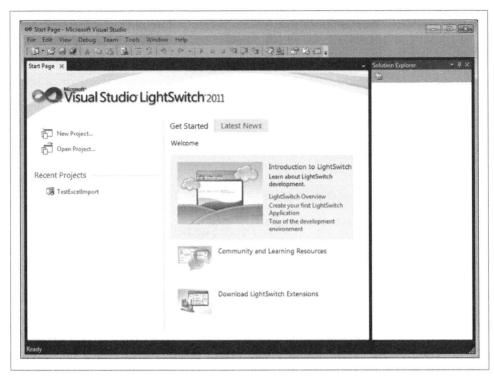

Figure 2-14. Main Screen for Visual Studio LightSwitch 2011

Summary

In this chapter, I presented multiple ways to configure both a server and workstation to facilitate developing Visual Studio LightSwitch applications with SharePoint. You should be good to go if you've followed along. It's important to note at this point that you won't be able to complete most of the sample applications presented in later chapters without a properly configured environment.

Simple Applications

With Visual Studio LightSwitch, it is extremely easy to build simple, single-function applications. This chapter will focus on these types of apps and how you can get them built and tested quickly. I'll walk you through the steps of connecting to a SharePoint site, as that will be required for most of the other examples in the book.

The first thing I want to do is talk about what you can do with the product. Connecting to some type of data source is a primary requirement for most business applications, and Visual Studio LightSwitch makes this the first thing you see when starting a new app. Making the process simple is where LightSwitch really shines.

With version 1.0, you have three basic options for connecting to an external data source: a database (meaning any installed ADO.NET provider), a SharePoint site, or a Windows Communication Foundation (WCF) Rich Internet Application (RIA) Service. You also have the option of creating a new table from scratch. Visual Studio LightSwitch is a great tool for building simple database applications using SQL Server Express 2008 as the underlying engine.

We'll spend the rest of the book talking about option two since this book is about building SharePoint applications with Visual Studio LightSwitch. With option three or WCF RIA services, you have the ability to connect to a wide variety of data sources, including any source supporting the OData protocol. This approach is definitely the most complex of the three, but with the complexity comes great flexibility.

Utility Functions

Connecting to a SharePoint site is supported as one of the three primary external data choices, as shown in Figure 3-1.

When you click Next from this dialog, you'll have the chance to specify the URL address of your SharePoint site. Figure 3-2 shows what this dialog looks like.

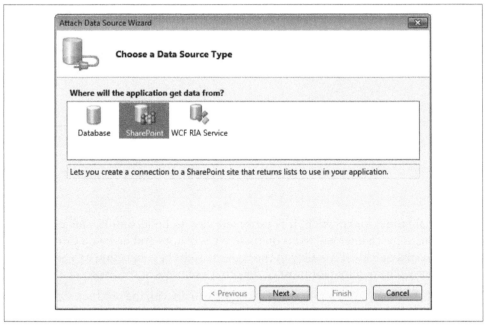

Figure 3-1. External data source options

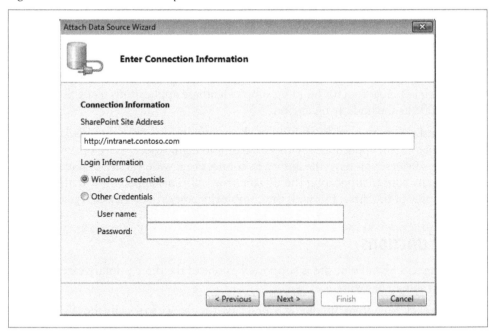

Figure 3-2. SharePoint URL connection dialog

For the purposes of this demo, we'll stick with the user's Windows credentials, although you could use some other credentials if you needed to. This might be needed in the case of obtaining elevated privileges or to test limited privileges. Clicking Next here will attempt to make the connection to the SharePoint site and retrieve all the available lists. If you've worked with SharePoint before, you should recognize many of the list names. You can choose to keep the default name of Team_SiteData or change it to something else.

There will be one item selected by default in the list of SharePoint items, as shown in Figure 3-3. This list is named UserInformationList, and it contains all the information stored on each SharePoint user. All other lists are linked to the UserInformationList as they contain the "Created by" and "Modified by" fields, which point to a specific user.

One thing to note here about users: the UserInformationList does not necessarily contain every domain user unless that user has actually connected to the SharePoint site. To populate the UserInformationList, you must log into the client machine using different domain users and the default password (pass@word1). Next, use Internet Explorer to open the *http://intranet.contoso.com* site to actually register that user.

For the first LightSwitch example application, we're going to build a simple user browser tool. We don't need any other lists besides the UserInformationList, as it contains everything we need to view registered users.

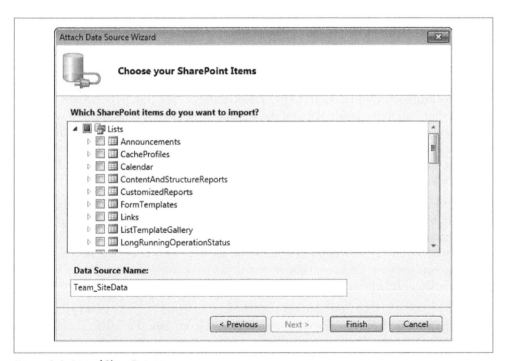

Figure 3-3. List of SharePoint items

When you click Finish, LightSwitch will build an initial solution and present a screen like the one in Figure 3-4.

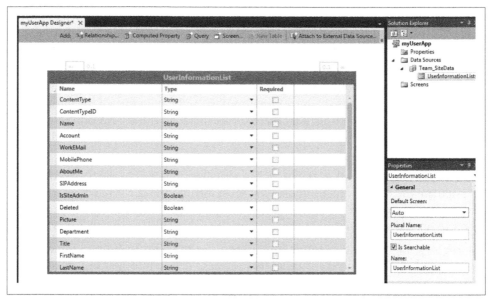

Figure 3-4. Initial application screen

From here you can modify the default settings for the fields in the linked table or press on to adding user screens. In later examples, it will be necessary to make changes to some fields such as Date Time values to modify how they appear on the screen. This will make more sense when we get to the Tasks example. We'll skip the default settings at this point and move on to defining the screens. You have several ways in which to add a new screen to your project. One way is to click the Screen button at the top of the page or use the key combination Ctrl-Shift-E. You can also right-click on the Screens folder in the Solution Explorer window on the righthand side of the screen and choose Add Screen.

You should see a dialog like the one shown in Figure 3-5 appear next. This dialog shows the available screen templates on the lefthand side, a simple example of what the selected template will look like, and all available data sources or queries on the righthand side. Visual Studio LightSwitch will generate all the necessary code to connect the data to the screen for you. The downside is you don't have a lot of control over how the screen looks, although we will look at some of the things that can be modified a little later.

At this point, you have five screen types to choose from (see the lefthand column in Figure 3-5). You also have the opportunity to change the name of the screen in the Screen Name box should you wish to do so. You'll need to choose what data will connect to this screen by choosing from the options under Screen Data. For this

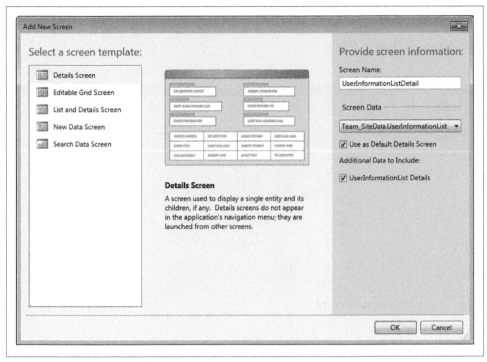

Figure 3-5. Add New Screen dialog

example, there should only be one table, as we did not select any others during the application creation process. For this sample application, we're going to pick the Editable Grid Screen.

If you've followed along to this point, you should be able to build and run your application by either clicking the Run button (green arrow button) or by pressing the F5 key. This will display the default fields in a grid like the one shown in Figure 3-6. You can see at this point that the default fields shown on this screen don't really display the information we would like shown. Another issue is that there are groups displayed along with "Person" content types. We'll need to add a few things to clean this up some.

The key idea here is that Visual Studio LightSwitch will build a working application for you based on taking all the defaults for your data source and screen. What results from taking the defaults is probably not what you wanted. There will be some tweaking required to get the information we want to see on the screen. That's what we'll look at next.

Changing the columns displayed can be done from the screen designer tool. This is where you would add additional fields besides the default ones added for you by Visual Studio LightSwitch. To bring it up, you will need to exit your running application and then double-click on the EditableUserInformationListsGrid item under the Screens folder in the Solution Explorer. This will present the designer in a three-pane screen with the UserInformationLists fields in the lefthand pane and the current screen definition in the middle. The righthand pane has the Solution Explorer and the Properties pane (see Figure 3-7).

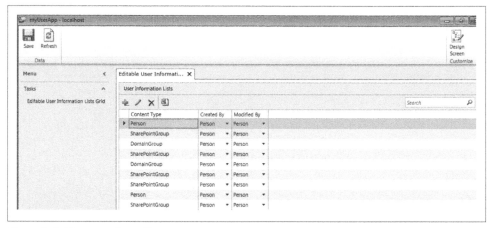

Figure 3-6. First run of user list app

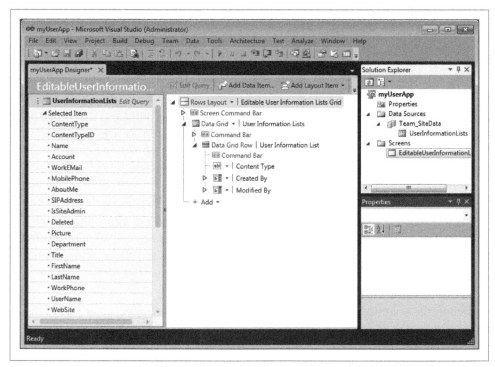

Figure 3-7. Visual Studio LightSwitch screen designer

To delete existing fields, you can either right-click on the field—such as Content Type—and choose Delete, or simply highlight the field and press the Delete key. To add any of the fields from the UserInformationLists, simply click on the field, drag it into the list of field names, and drop it in the position you want it to appear. LightSwitch helps out with blue guide lines to show you where the field will be placed when you release the mouse button.

Notice the Design Screen Customize button in the top-righthand corner of the application window (from Figure 3-6). This gives you the option to customize the look and feel of the screen while it's running. Clicking on this button will bring up a new dialog like the one shown in Figure 3-8.

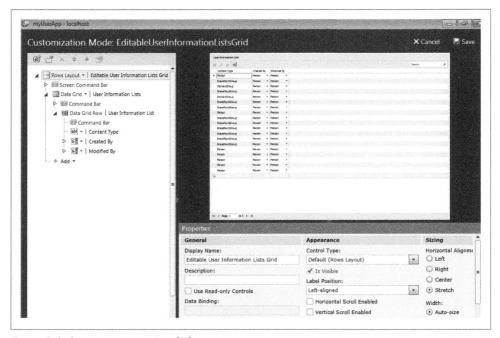

Figure 3-8. Screen customization dialog

From here you have the ability to change everything about the screen while viewing what the screen will look like. You can delete fields from the lefthand screen by selecting the field and pressing the Delete key. To add new fields, click the Add label and select the desired item. For this demo, let's delete the three default fields and add Name, Work e-mail, Work phone, Title, and Department.

Figure 3-9. Query builder dialog screen

The last thing we're going to do for this sample is to create a query to only show actual user information. To do this, click on the blue Edit Query label at the top of the lefthand pane next to the UserInformationLists label (see Figure 3-7). This will bring up a query builder dialog as shown in Figure 3-9.

To add a filter expression, click Add Filter, and you should see a new line appear like the one shown in Figure 3-10. In order to display only users, we need to choose the ContentType field to filter on and then enter **Person** in the final text box.

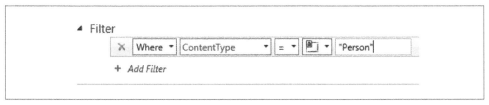

Figure 3-10. Filter query details

Now we should be ready to run the application and see a list of all users registered with the SharePoint site. Figure 3-11 shows our app in its current state.

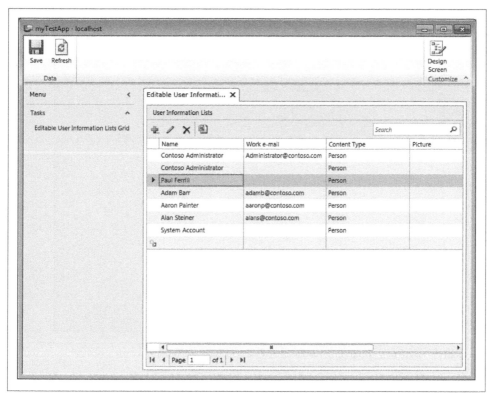

Figure 3-11. User list application

Search Tools

One of the things that SharePoint is really good at is search. Many organizations implement SharePoint as a way of making it possible to find information stored either in lists or in other content managed by SharePoint. Building a simple search tool should be fairly straightforward.

One of the options when you create a new screen is a Search Data Screen (as shown in Figure 3-5). This will create a screen with a list of default fields and a search box. Adding a search data screen and taking the defaults for our previous user list app will create a screen that looks something like Figure 3-12.

Visual Studio LightSwitch will create the code to search the underlying data connection using the text in the Search box. Any of the displayed text fields are searchable.

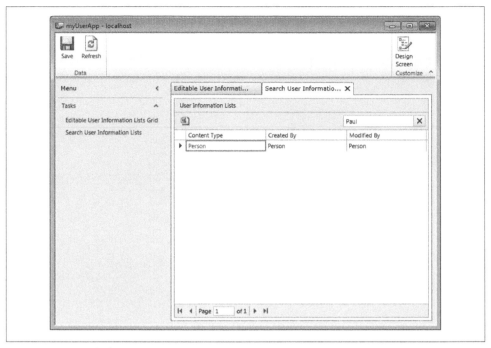

Figure 3-12. Search data screen

The key to building custom search screens lies in building parameterized queries. Adding a query against any data connection is drop-dead simple. The easiest way to do this is to right-click on the data connection name in the Solution Explorer and choose Add Query. This will bring up the query builder design screen previously shown in Figure 3-9. This time, we're going to create a new filter based on a parameter. With the query builder open, let's specify a new title of User Name.

Next we need to change the type of query to parameter and give it a name. Visual Studio LightSwitch will prompt you with Add New to allow you to create a new named parameter. For this query, let's use UserName as the parameter and then save the query. Now we can create a new search screen and use the query as the data source. One thing to point out here is that Visual Studio LightSwitch will, by default, execute all queries each time you change the criteria field unless you uncheck the box labeled Auto Execute Query in the properties page for the query.

We'll generate a unique query to filter by department or search by name. Figure 3-13 shows what the final search tool should look like.

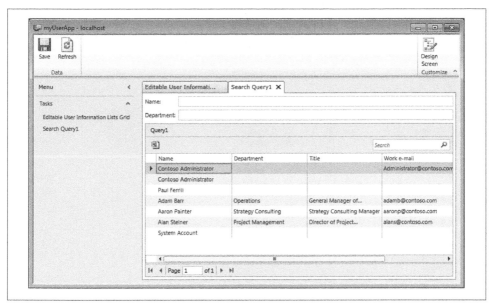

Figure 3-13. Search tool with query parameters

Data Entry

Creating user screens with Visual Studio LightSwitch is about as easy as it gets. For this example, we're going to create a simple data entry application attached to the Share-Point Tasks list. This will allow us to quickly enter, display, and edit information about all existing tasks.

The first thing we have to do is create a new solution and connect to the Task list using the same process shown at the beginning of this chapter. When that's complete, you should have a screen that looks something like Figure 3-14. Visual Studio LightSwitch will bring over the types for each element from SharePoint, but you can change how they are presented should you so choose. For this application, we'll change the Start Date and Due Date fields to a type of date rather than date-time. This is more appropriate for entry and will simplify the screen as well.

For the final screen display, we don't really need all the fields from the Task list. To clean things up, I removed Content Type plus everything after Due Date.

Now we need to build the actual data entry screen. This is a good place to talk about a few features in Visual Studio LightSwitch that help make building this type of application simple. The first feature we'll look at is field validation. There are a number of predefined field types, such as phone, e-mail, social security number, and ZIP code. You can choose to use the canned validation routines or write your own.

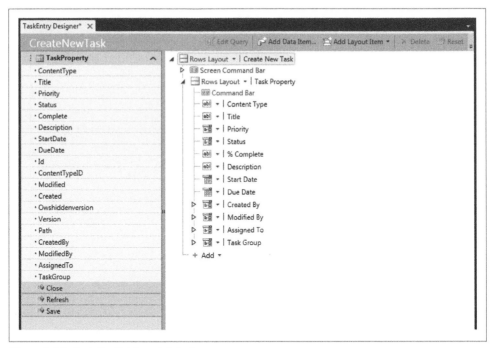

Figure 3-14. Task list fields and default screen

Another feature of Visual Studio LightSwitch is how it automatically builds things like choice lists from SharePoint fields with a fixed set of options. As an example, the Priority field of the Task list is a choice field with three possible options: High (1), Normal (2), and Low (3). When you build a screen connected to this field, it will use a prepopulated drop-down list.

We'll need to make a few changes to the default LightSwitch fields to make the data entry process a little smoother. To remove a field from being displayed on the screen, simply uncheck the Display by Default checkbox in the properties table (shown in Figure 3-15). It's a good idea to auto-populate fields, such as the Created By field, where you know what the value should be. Entering default values in fields for things like Start Date can improve usability as well.

Figure 3-16 shows how our final task data entry app looks. The final version uses a List and Details screen to show a list of tasks in a grid with the details beside it. Notice that you have two ways to add a new task using either the plus button or the Create New Task menu item.

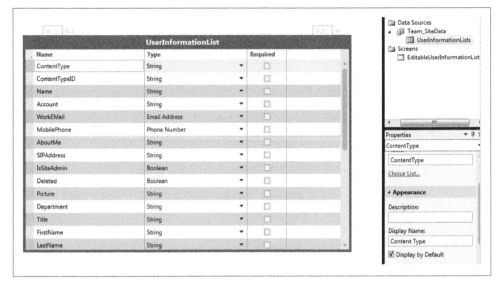

Figure 3-15. Display by Default checkbox

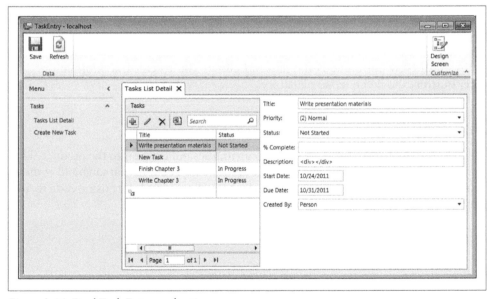

Figure 3-16. Final Task Entry application

Another place where you can do data entry is from a search screen. Let's show that by adding a few buttons to our user search app that we created earlier. To do that, click the Add button below the Data Grid Command Bar. You should see a drop-down list like the one in Figure 3-17.

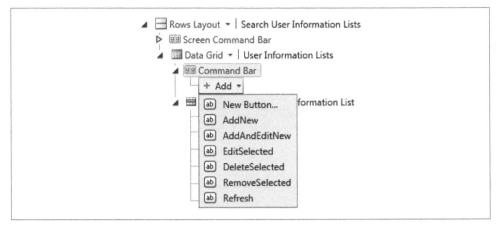

Figure 3-17. Adding command buttons to the search screen

Visual Studio LightSwitch supports six command buttons for managing records in a grid view. The first button, AddNew, only adds a blank line to the database, while the AddAndEditNew button adds the line and allows you to edit the information. The other buttons should be self-explanatory.

Summary

Visual Studio LightSwitch has a wealth of capabilities built right into the product. This chapter has just scratched the surface of the kinds of applications you can build without writing any code. I'll dig a little deeper in the next chapter and start using code to add even more functionality.

CHAPTER 4

Power User Applications

In this chapter, I'm going to dive deeper into building applications with more functionality. In reality, that means I'll be writing some code to make these sample apps do more when it comes to filtering and displaying data. While Visual Studio LightSwitch supports both C# and Visual Basic, I'll be using Visual Basic for all the code examples.

I'll also introduce you to LightSwitch extensions and using Silverlight to spruce things up a bit. Extensions make it possible to add features to Visual Studio LightSwitch to enhance the out-of-the-box capabilities. Examples I'll be using include the LightSwitch Filter control extension for filtering query results. In Chapter 5, I'll use the Excel export extension for two separate examples. Both of these free extensions are available on the Microsoft Visual Studio Gallery website under the LightSwitch section (*http://visual studiogallery.msdn.microsoft.com/*).

On the same site, you'll find an entire third-party ecosystem built around extensions for mainstream Visual Studio. Many of those same vendors are adapting their products for use with LightSwitch. I'll use one of those in Chapter 5 to connect to a Google data source. Microsoft provided a cookbook for developing Visual Studio LightSwitch extensions during the beta period of the product and now offers a number of tutorials and samples to help you write your own.

Administration Tools

One of the things we will need in most of the applications in this chapter is the ability to authenticate users to SharePoint. To do this, we'll be using basic Windows authentication to get access to the current logged-in user. To set this for any LightSwitch application, you simply select the "Use Windows authentication" radio button on the Access Control tab of the solution properties page, as shown in Figure 4-1.

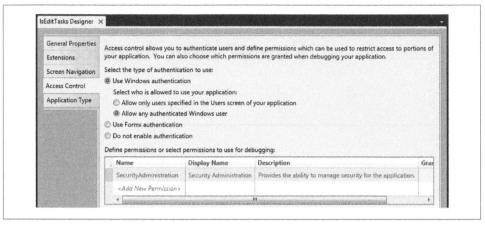

Figure 4-1. LightSwitch Solution Properties page

If you choose "Allow only users specified in the Users screen of your application," you'll have to maintain a list of users in the application. LightSwitch supports both entity- and screen-level permissions. In code, you will use a permission object, which must be defined in the Application Designer. Individual permissions are set by the application administrator. You can enable the administrator functionality temporarily by enabling the Granted for Debug checkbox for the Security Administration username. With that box checked, you'll see a new menu item when you run the application for administering Users and Roles (see Figure 4-2). This method does give you lots of flexibility but could get unwieldy with lots of users.

Figure 4-2. Administration menu

The other side of the permissions coin concerns the SharePoint site. You must connect to the site as a user with Create permissions, or you won't be able to make any changes. With that in mind, we're going to create a sample app that will make it easy to browse the current SharePoint user database and make any necessary changes. We'll start with a connection to the demo SharePoint site and the UserInformationList. Next, we'll create a screen using the Editable Grid template. We'll add a simple filter query to show just ContentType of Person. You should see something like Figure 4-3 at this point.

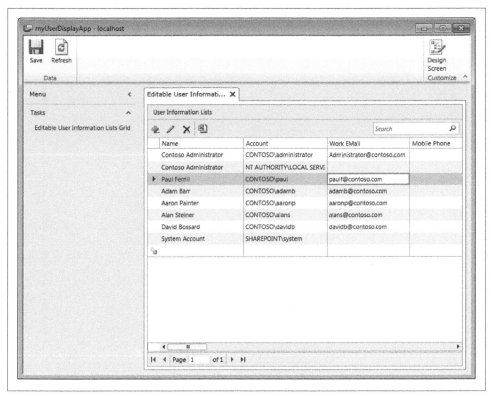

Figure 4-3. Editable grid showing contents of the UserInformationList

All columns in a LightSwitch grid are sortable if you click on the column header. This might not be obvious just looking at the grid, so you would want to document this for your users. The stock search box will search any string field across the entire dataset. If you need to search for some other field type like a phone number or a date, you'll either have to add some additional code or use something like a parameterized query to make it work.

Making Bulk Changes

If you've ever had to administer a SharePoint site before, you've probably been presented with the "ownership change" problem. It's not uncommon in organizations of all sizes to have an employee leave. The problem is what to do with things like SharePoint lists or tasks assigned to them. An obvious solution is to write a program to make the changes for you.

We'll use the task application from the previous chapter as a starting point and add some functionality to implement a search-and-replace capability. The basic approach is to build a search screen to find all items assigned to a specific user and then add code behind a button to change the owner to a different user. Figure 4-4 shows what the basic app looks like.

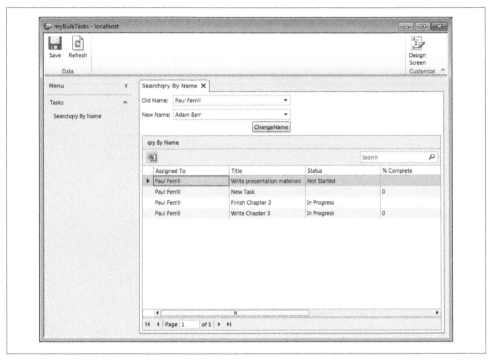

Figure 4-4. Bulk task ownership change app

There are a few steps required to make this app work. The app uses an external connection to the demo SharePoint site with the Tasks and UserInformationList lists selected. With these two data sources available, we'll need to add a parameterized query to search for all tasks assigned to a specific person.

First of all, we need to add the two list boxes at the top of the screen labeled Old Name and New Name. This is done by clicking the Add Data Item button, as shown in Figure 4-5.

Figure 4-5. Add Data Item button at the top of the screen designer page

This will bring up a dialog box like the one in Figure 4-6. In order to add a new list box element to the screen, we must choose Local Property and then select Team_Site-Data.UserInformationList.

Now that we have the data elements defined, we need to work on the screen layout. Visual Studio LightSwitch will set all screen elements to autosize by default. While this works just fine in most cases, it will cause some elements like list or text boxes to be larger than needed. The best way to make these changes is to first run the application and then modify the screen using the Design Screen option (see Figure 3-6 in Chapter 3).

Once we have the data element defined, it needs to be connected to the query parameter so that selecting a name from the drop-down list changes the displayed task items appropriately. Visual Studio LightSwitch adds a data item with the name of the parameter when you initially define the query. We will be using the new data item for this purpose, so you can just delete the account item. To add the data item to the screen, simply click and drag it from the lefthand pane onto the screen tree-view just below the command bar.

The last step is to set the Parameter Binding property of the account query parameter to OldName.Account, as shown in Figure 4-7. This will connect the UserInformationList-based list of user names to the drop-down list box on our screen.

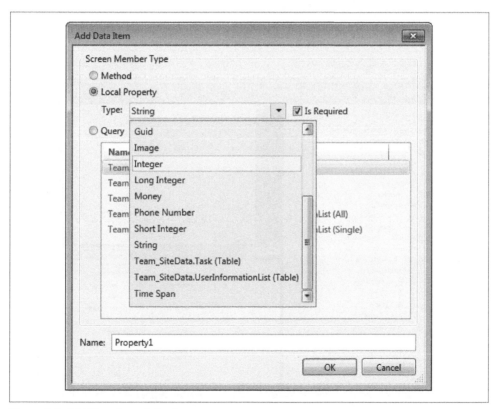

Figure 4-6. Add Data Item dialog box

Figure 4-7. Parameter Binding property page

You will need to click the Design Screen button in order to change the way specific elements display on the screen. We'll use this method to change the size of the two list boxes so they don't take up the entire screen. Figure 4-8 shows the design screen with Old Name selected in the element tree on the lefthand side of the screen. To set the width to a fixed value, you must choose either Pixels or Characters and then enter an appropriate value.

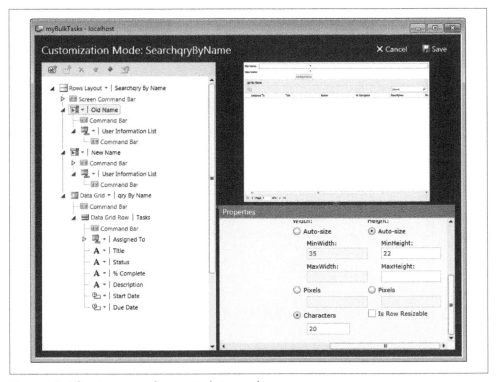

Figure 4-8. Adjusting screen elements in design mode

LightSwitch Extensions

One of the great features available with Visual Studio LightSwitch is the ability to expand the out-of-the-box capabilities with extensions. Microsoft provides several free sample extensions on the Visual Studio LightSwitch website along with both user-contributed and commercial extensions. In this section, we'll look at one of the Microsoft extensions, the LightSwitch filter control, and then use another extension to wrap up this chapter. You can create your own extensions as well by downloading the Visual Studio LightSwitch Extensibility Toolkit.

For this example, you'll need to download the LightSwitch Filter Control from the Visual Studio Samples website (*http://code.msdn.microsoft.com/Filter-Control-for-Vis ual-90fb8e93*). Once you have the project downloaded, you'll need to extract the files and run the *.vsix* file to install it. It should be in the Binaries subdirectory. To use the extension in a project, you must enable it on the project properties page, as shown in Figure 4-9.

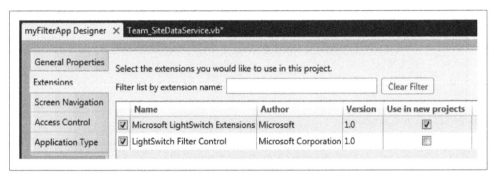

Figure 4-9. Enable LightSwitch Filter Control on the extensions tab

The steps to create a screen that will use this extension are as follows. First, start a new project, then connect to the SharePoint demo site and the UserInformationList. Next, open a query tab and simply add a parameter using the Add Query Element dropdown, as shown in Figure 4-10. We'll name the query `filterByQuery` and the parameter `FilterString`.

The only line of code required to use the Filter Extension must go in the `filterBy Query_PreprocessQuery` routine. To access this code from the query designer, click on the Write Code dropdown and select `filterByQuery_PreprocessQuery`. This will present a code screen like the one in Figure 4-11. Add the following line of code:

```
query = LightSwitchFIlter.Server.Filter(query, FilterString, Me.Application)
```

Now we'll add a screen based on the query we just created. The quickest way to do this is to right-click on the Screens folder in the righthand Solution Explorer screen and choose Add Screen. From here, we want to add a Search screen and link it to the

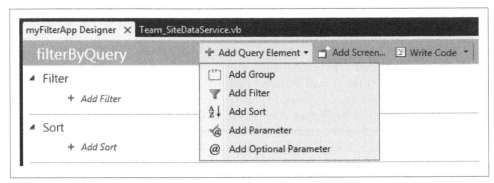

Figure 4-10. Add Parameter from the Query designer

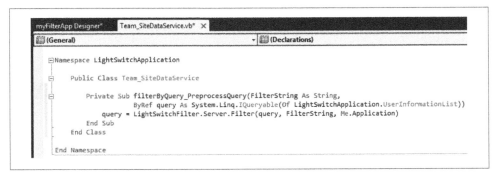

Figure 4-11. Code behind query

`filterByQuery` data source. In order to use the Filter Extension, you must change the control created by LightSwitch to the Advanced Filter Builder, as shown in Figure 4-12.

There's one last thing you'll want to do to make this application a little more useful. On the screen designer page, you must check the box labeled Display Report Save Options under Properties for the Advanced Filter Builder. It's not checked by default, although you'll want to check it to provide the option of saving queries.

The full code base of the extension comes with the project when you download the zip file. You will need to have the full version of Visual Studio Professional 2010 with Service Pack 1 (SP1) plus the Visual Studio SDK and LightSwitch Extensions toolkit in order to build the sample code. This sample provides a good example to show you how an operational extension works and what's needed to build your own.

All that's left now is to run the application. The final version should look like what's shown in Figure 4-13. Notice that the top of the screen now has a number of new controls to build new queries on the fly based on any field in the attached data source. You can also save queries for later use with the Save button. The code behind the Save button is a good example of how to save information to the local file system. You can also see an example of using the `IsolatedStorageFile` routine to load previously saved queries.

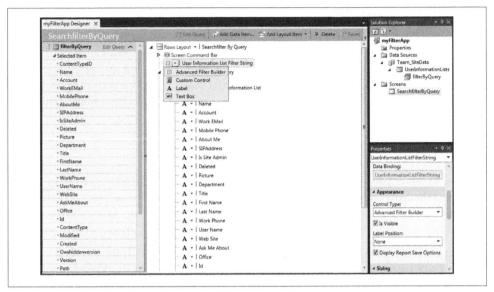

Figure 4-12. Select the Advanced Filter Builder control on the screen

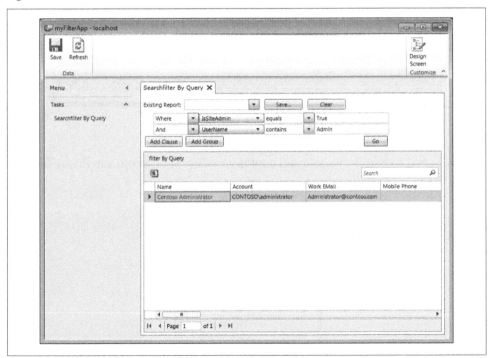

Figure 4-13. Final version of the Filter Extension sample app

Silverlight Controls

Another way to expand the capabilities of Visual Studio LightSwitch is through the use of Silverlight Controls. The only downside here is that you'll need a full version of Visual Studio Professional with SP1installed in order to take advantage of this feature. Microsoft does offer several ways to try out Visual Studio without actually purchasing the product, including a 30-day trial version (*http://www.microsoft.com/visualstudio/en-us/try*).

That being said, I'm going to show you how to build an app that uses a Silverlight Chart control to show task completion in a bar graph.

For this sample, you'll need to download and install the Silverlight 4.0 toolkit. You'll find it on the Microsoft Code project site (*http://silverlight.codeplex.com*). The basis of this example will be a LightSwitch project attached to the demo SharePoint site and the Tasks list. We'll also need a parameterized query to return all tasks by username.

Adding a Silverlight control to a LightSwitch project is not hard. First, you'll need to add a new Silverlight class library solution to the project using the New Project item on the File Menu. We want to add this to our current solution, so change the "Solution:" item to "Add to solution" (see Figure 4-14).

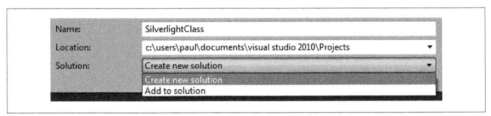

Figure 4-14. "Add to solution option" from Add New Project

Now we need to switch the solution explorer to display all project items by file (see Figure 4-15).

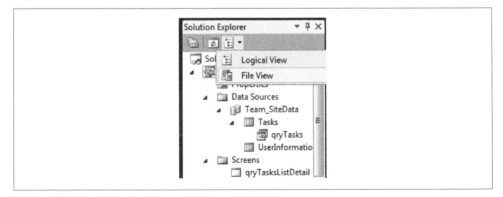

Figure 4-15. Visual Studio Solution Explorer in File View

This makes it easy to see the actual files that make up the project. We need to delete the *Class1.vb* file, as we won't be needing it for this project. Next, right-click on Silverlight Class and choose Add – New Item. From the New Item dialog, choose Silverlight User Control and name it **ChartControl.xaml**. At this point, you should see a design surface similar to the one shown in Figure 4-16.

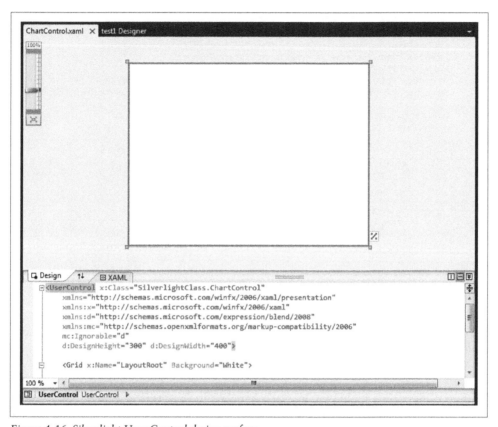

Figure 4-16. Silverlight User Control design surface

 If you don't see the Toolbox on your screen, you can use the key combination Control-Alt-X to bring it forward.

Now you must drag a Silverlight Chart control onto the design surface. Resize it to fill the entire box. At this point, you have a Silverlight User Control available to be used in your LightSwitch application. There are a few things we need to add to the XAML to connect to the screen data. The XAML code needed to accomplish the next step is not documented anywhere on the Microsoft LightSwitch site, but it is available if you do a little searching in the LightSwitch support forums.

It's necessary to make a connection between the Silverlight screen and the data returned by the LightSwitch query. Figure 4-17 shows what the XAML file looks like after adding the additional XAML code.

```xml
<UserControl x:Class="SilverlightClass.ChartControl"
    xmlns="http://schemas.microsoft.com/winfx/2006/xaml/presentation"
    xmlns:x="http://schemas.microsoft.com/winfx/2006/xaml"
    xmlns:d="http://schemas.microsoft.com/expression/blend/2008"
    xmlns:mc="http://schemas.openxmlformats.org/markup-compatibility/2006"
    xmlns:toolkit="http://schemas.microsoft.com/winfx/2006/xaml/presentation/toolkit">

    <Grid x:Name="LayoutRoot" Background="White">
        <toolkit:Chart HorizontalAlignment="Left" Name="Chart1"
                        Title="Task Completion"
                        VerticalAlignment="Top" Height="300" Width="400">
            <toolkit:Chart.LegendStyle>
                <Style TargetType="toolkit:Legend">
                    <Setter Property="Width" Value = "0"/>
                    <Setter Property="Height" Value = "0"/>
                </Style>
            </toolkit:Chart.LegendStyle>
            <toolkit:ColumnSeries ItemsSource="{Binding Screen.qryTasks}"
                                DependentValueBinding="{Binding Complete}"
                                IndependentValueBinding="{Binding Title}">

            </toolkit:ColumnSeries>
        </toolkit:Chart>
    </Grid>
</UserControl>
```

Figure 4-17. XAML for Silverlight Chart control

Binding to data on a LightSwitch screen happens in the ItemsSource tag. In essence, we're going to bind to the qryTasks entity on the LightSwitch Screen. For the Depend entValue of the chart, or the legend across the side, we will use the Complete field from qryTasks. The IndependentValue, or legend across the bottom, will link to the task Title field. The only other change to the XAML file is the section under the Chart.Legend Style tag. This is an option to turn off the chart legend that would otherwise show by default. Go ahead and build the project here to make the Silverlight class available to LightSwitch.

At this point, we're ready to add the user control to our LightSwitch screen. All that has to be done now is to click Add label at the bottom of the Screen Designer (shown in Figure 4-18). When you choose User Control, you should see a dialog with a list of available controls. First, we need to add a reference to our Silverlight Class using the Add Reference button. You should see it on the Projects tab.

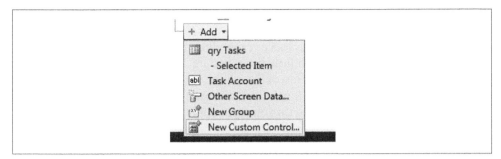

Figure 4-18. Add New Custom Control to LightSwitch screen

Once that's done, you should be able to change any of the screen characteristics of the control such as height/width. Figure 4-19 shows what our final application looks like.

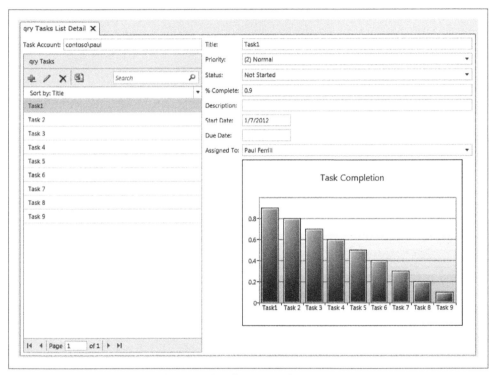

Figure 4-19. Task Detail list with Silverlight Chart control

Summary

Visual Studio LightSwitch provides lots of capabilities out of the box. The good news is you can expand on those with a little bit of coding and the use of other resources, such as extensions. With the addition of Silverlight, you can build user interfaces with virtually unlimited functionality. Hopefully, these examples have prompted a few ideas of your own to help you get started on your next application.

CHAPTER 5

Application Integration

For this final chapter, I will address connecting a LightSwitch application to multiple external data sources, starting with Excel files. It's a pretty safe assumption that where you find Microsoft SharePoint, you'll also find Microsoft Office. Exporting data to Microsoft Excel is a built-in capability of the product. Importing data from either Excel or a comma separated value (CSV) file requires an extension but brings with it some added functionality. Having the ability to both import and export data makes it possible to move data between different systems.

Using Microsoft SQL Server Express 2008 for the underlying database is fine if you have total control over the data, but it's not an uncommon task to need to connect to other databases. I'll show you how to directly connect to a SQLite database using a freely available download. The other big topic for this chapter is integrating with cloud services like Google. While you could write a lot of code to connect with Google Calendar, I'll be using a third-party extension that only requires a few lines of code to implement.

Easy Excel Integration

For this example, we're going to build a sample app that connects to the Calendar list of our demo SharePoint site. The cool part of this example is the ability to import a list of calendar events from Excel. To get started, we'll follow the same basic process of creating a new Visual Studio LightSwitch app as in the previous chapters, with the exception of connecting to the Calendar list instead of Tasks. With the Calendar list schema screen displayed, you will need to change the Summary Property to Title (see Figure 5-1).

For the user screen, we'll add an Editable Grid connected to the Calendar list. Go ahead and build/run the app. Visual Studio LightSwitch provides a basic export capability in the form of a button (it looks like an Excel icon) to send all currently displayed records to an Excel file. When you click the button, you should see Microsoft Excel open with the records displayed on a sheet named Calendars. This only works if you have

Figure 5-1. Summary property of the Calendar data source

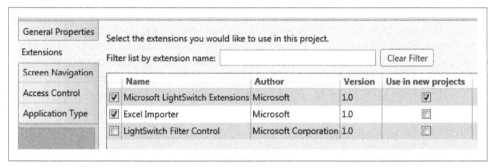

Figure 5-2. Application Properties page and the Extensions tab

Microsoft Excel installed on the local machine, as it uses COM Interop to attempt to launch the program. The next step is to reverse the process and import data from an Excel file.

The good news here is there's an extension for handling everything with regard to importing an Excel file, including all file mapping. It's available on the Microsoft MSDN site (*http://code.msdn.microsoft.com/silverlight/Excel-Importer-for-Visual-61dd4a90*). The latest version even supports CSV files. Once the zip file has downloaded, you'll need to unpack it and install the extension by executing the vsix file found in the Binaries directory.

Next you'll need to enable the extension on the Properties page for the application.

Back on the Editable Grid screen, we need to add a button to implement the import capability. To do this, you can right-click on the Command Bar just below the Data Grid line and select Add Button. For this demo, we'll name the button **ImportFromExcel**. The last thing we need to do is add a single line of code to launch the import tool.

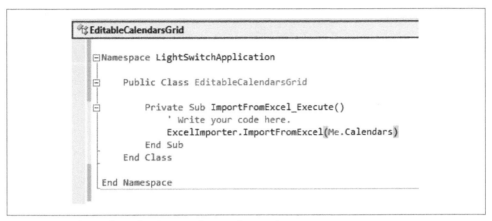

```
EditableCalendarsGrid

Namespace LightSwitchApplication

    Public Class EditableCalendarsGrid

        Private Sub ImportFromExcel_Execute()
            ' Write your code here.
            ExcelImporter.ImportFromExcel(Me.Calendars)
        End Sub
    End Class

End Namespace
```

Figure 5-3. Only one line of code to implement the Excel import

To add the code, right-click on the button and choose Edit Execute Code. This will open a new window with default code like the one shown in Figure 5-3. The one line of code is just after the line ' Write your code here. ExcelImporter.ImportFromExcel takes exactly one parameter, which is the screen collection (Me.Calendars).

The easiest way to create an Excel file with the appropriate columns is to use the built-in LightSwitch Excel export tool. For the example calendar data, you will get a file that looks something like Figure 5-4.

	A	B	C	D	E	F	G	H	I	J	K
	Title	Location	Start Time	End Time	Description	All Day Event	Recurrence	Workspace	Category	Created By	Modified By
	Chapter 3 Due		1/2/2012 12:00:00 AM	1/2/2012 11:59:00 PM		True				Person	Person
	Chapter 4 Due		1/9/2012 12:00:00 AM	1/9/2012 11:59:00 PM		True	False	False		Person	Person
	Travel to Customer Site		1/16/2012 12:00:00 AM	1/20/2012 11:59:00 PM		True	False	False		Person	Person
	Final Chapter Due		1/23/2012 12:00:00 AM	1/23/2012 11:59:00 PM		True	False	False		Person	Person

Figure 5-4. Sample Excel export file

To create a new file to use for import, simply add a few new rows and then delete the first four rows with data. Now we're ready to run the app and import some data. Figure 5-5 shows what the application should look like when run.

When you click the Import From Excel button, you'll first see an open file dialog followed by a dialog for field mapping (see Figure 5-6). The last dialog allows you to map the fields in your import file to the fields in your database. In this case, we used a file previously exported from our application, meaning the fields should map one-for-one.

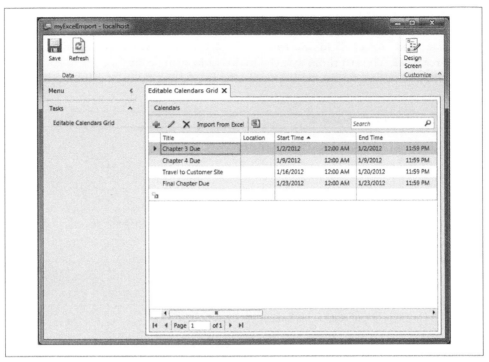

Figure 5-5. Final app with Import From Excel button

Figure 5-6. Field mapping dialog

Clicking the Continue button should show the new rows added to the bottom of your grid. Don't forget to click the Save button if you want to update the data to SharePoint as well.

The Excel Importer extension is a great way to get Excel data into your application without a lot of effort. You can also learn a lot about writing your own extensions since the source code for the entire extension is available. If you do examine the code, you'll see that there are even more capabilities with this extension than Excel files.

Data Import/Export

Getting data into and out of a Visual Studio LightSwitch application isn't hard but does require some coding. At a very high level, we'll add a button to a LightSwitch form and then add code behind the button to do the dirty work. In this example, I'll use a grid for the basic on-screen display tool and then export/import data through the rows of the grid.

We'll use a slight variation of our previous myTask app as the starting point but add the ability to read in a CSV file with new tasks. Make sure to change the summary property of the Tasks table to Title and the UserInformationList to Name. The key here is the use of the Excel extension referenced previously in this chapter. The good news here is that it will also import CSV files. We're going to add more information by using the current user name to attach to the Task Created By field.

Here's what the CSV file we'll be importing looks like:

```
Title,Start Date,Due Date
Initiate Proposal Process,12/30/2011,1/20/2012
First Draft Due,1/20/2012,2/3/2012
Form Proposal Team,12/30/2011,1/6/2012
Start Project,12/30/2011,3/2/2012
Team Kickoff Meeting, 1/6/2012, 1/6/2012
Team Status Meeting #1,1/13/2012,1/13/2012
Team Status Meeting #2,1/20/2012,1/20/2012
```

Notice the first line has field names and match the field names of the Tasks list. This will make it easy to pair the fields between the import file and the target Task list when we run the program.

To get started, we'll use our standard approach with a connection to the demo Share-Point site and the Task list. Then we'll create a screen using the Editable Grid template and finally add a button to implement the import. You need to change the summary property on the task table to Title and on the UserInformationList to Account. We'll also change the data types for the two date fields to Date instead of Date Time. As in the previous example, you'll have to open the Properties page to make the Excel Importer extension available.

Now we're ready to add a button and a few lines of code. Make sure the Editable TasksGrid is currently shown on the screen and then right-click on the Command Bar label just below the Data Grid. Select the Add button and name the method **ImportData**. With the new button displayed, open up the code window by either double-clicking or right-clicking on the button and choosing Edit Execute Code. Here we'll add the line to launch the Excel Importer tool with one line of code as follows:

```
ExcelImporter.Importer.ImportFromExcel(Me.Tasks)
```

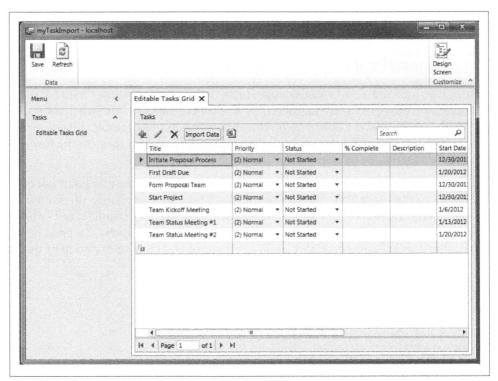

Figure 5-7. Task Import screen

There's one more place where we'll add a few lines of code to update the CreatedBy field, and that's in the `EditableTasksGrid_Saving` routine. This routine is called when you click the Save button. Figure 5-7 shows how the final version of the app should look.

```
Private Sub EditableTasksGrid_Saving(ByRef handled As Boolean)
    ' Write your code here.
    For Each tsk As Task In Me.DataWorkspace.HomeData.Details.GetChanges()_
            .OfType(Of Task)()
        tsk.CreatedBy.Name = Me.Application.User.Name
    Next
End Sub
```

This code will iterate over all changes and assign the current user's name to the CreatedBy field in each task. You could change other fields from this routine as well. Microsoft has a number of other examples in the article "Performing Data-Related

Tasks by Using Code" on the Visual Studio LightSwitch MSDN site (*http://msdn.mi crosoft.com/en-us/library/ff851990.aspx*).

Connecting with Other Databases

There are many other database engines besides Microsoft SQL. It's not uncommon to need to connect to, or at least import data from, some other database system. You could do it using the CSV method discussed earlier, or you could save a step and connect directly to the database. For this example, we'll take the last option and connect to a SQLite database.

To follow along with this example, you'll need to download the *System.Data.SQLite* package available from *http://sourceforge.net/projects/sqlite-dotnet2*. This page has a link to the ADO.NET 2.0/3.5 Provider for SQLite. Download and run the setup file to install the provider into Visual Studio.

Once this has been installed, you'll have a new option on the Attach Data Source Wizard for SQLite Database File (see Figure 5-8). If you search around a bit with Google, you should be able to find any number of different sample SQLite databases. There's even a sample of the NorthWind database available for testing, which I'll use for this example (*http://code.google.com/p/northwindextended/*).

The basic premise for this app is to query the SharePoint UserInformationList and then push the results out to a SQLite database. In theory, you could use the same technique to create an export/import or backup tool. For the purpose of this example, we'll use the previously created User Info task and add the capability to export information to a preexisting SQLite database file.

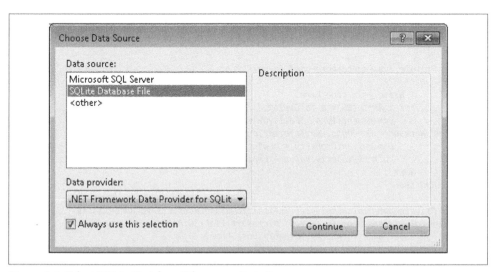

Figure 5-8. Select SQLite Database File as new Data Source

We'll use a single search screen for this application connected to the SQLite database. This type of screen has a basic search capability that will suffice for this example. The intent is to find a subset of employees in the SQLite database that we want to add to the SharePoint UserInformationList. Once you enter a search term, you will have an on-screen display of employees that we can use programmatically. Note that this technique works only with records shown on the screen.

The last thing we need is a button to put code behind. Open the screen designer for the search screen. Right-click on the Command Bar label and choose Add Button (See Figure 5-9). Name it **CopytoSharePoint**. You'll need to edit the Display Name property to get it to display on the screen properly. Change that to **Copy to SharePoint**.

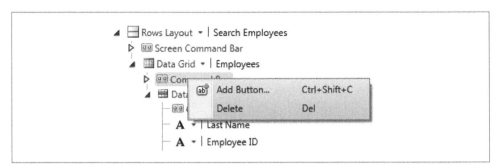

Figure 5-9. Add Button pop-up on Screen Designer

With the new button added, you simply double-click it to bring up the code window. The actual code is pretty simple and consists of a single *for* loop counting from zero to Employees.Count − 1. This will iterate over all employee records on the screen. Here's what the code looks like:

```
Public Class SearchEmployees

    Private Sub CopytoSharePoint_Execute()

        ' Write your code here.
        For i As Int16 = 0 To Employees.Count - 1
            Dim newEntity As IEntityObject = _
Me.DataWorkspace.HomeData.UserInformationLists.AddNew()
            Dim currentProperty = newEntity.Details.Properties("Name")
            currentProperty.Value = Employees(i).LastName
        Next i
    End Sub

    Private Sub SearchEmployees_InitializeDataWorkspace(saveChangesTo As _
System.Collections.Generic.List(Of Microsoft.LightSwitch.IDataService))
        saveChangesTo.Add(Me.DataWorkspace.HomeData)
    End Sub

    Private Sub SearchEmployees_Saving(ByRef handled As Boolean)
        Me.DataWorkspace.HomeData.SaveChanges()
```

```
        End Sub
    End Class
```

The final version of the app should look something like Figure 5-10. You can see the influence of the Entity Framework in this code. To add information to the UserInformationLists, you use the `AddNew()` method on the entity associated with that SharePoint list.

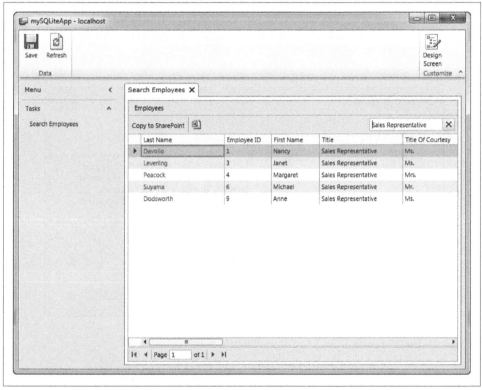

Figure 5-10. Final version of the SQLite app

Cloud-Based Application Integration

When it comes to integrating with cloud-based applications, there is one player that generally comes to mind first, and that would be Google. There is a demo version of a Google Data extension from RSSBus available from the Visual Studio LightSwitch gallery. We'll use this extension to show how easy it is to connect to literally any Google data source.

For this last example, we're going to build a simple tool that will query for calendar events and then give you the option of adding the event to a Google calendar. With the

RSSBus extension, you simply add a new data source and choose their provider (see Figure 5-11).

The Visual Studio LightSwitch site has links to a wide variety of extensions to meet just about any need. Most of the vendors offer time-limited trial versions of their products for you to try out before you buy (see *http://www.microsoft.com/visualstudio/en-us/lightswitch/extensions*).

If you don't find what you're looking for, you could always just write an extension yourself. Check out the LightSwitch Developer Center for downloads, examples and tutorials to help get you going (see *http://msdn.microsoft.com/en-us/lightswitch/hh304488*).

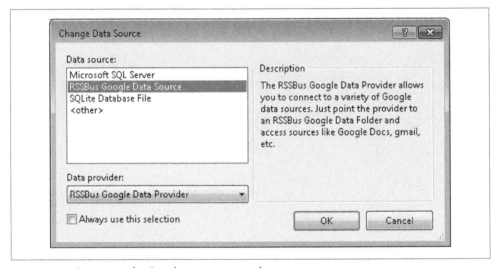

Figure 5-11. Connect to the Google extension as a data source

The Connection Properties page is where you set your Google username and password. This can also be set programmatically (see Figure 5-12).

Once you have the connection established, you should see a dialog similar to the one you see with SharePoint connections displaying the available Google data sources for you to choose from (see Figure 5-13).

We'll also connect to our SharePoint demo site and the Calendar list. From this list, we'll create a search screen allowing us to find calendar events to post to Google and then add a button to actually execute the move. All of this should be familiar to you by now, so I won't go over it again. Here's what the code looks like for the button:

Figure 5-12. Credentials can be set at design time or with code

```vb
Public Class SearchCalendar

    Private Sub SendtoGoogle_Execute()

        ' Write your code here.
        For i As Int16 = 0 To Me.Details.Screen.Calendars.Count - 1
            Dim gcal = Me.DataWorkspace.DataSource1.Calendars.AddNew()
            gcal.StartTime = Me.Details.Screen.Calendars(i).StartTime
            gcal.EndTime = Me.Details.Screen.Calendars(i).EndTime
            gcal.Title = Me.Details.Screen.Calendars(i).Title
            If IsNothing(Me.Details.Screen.Calendars(i).Description)
                gcal.Description = " "
            Else
                gcal.Description = Me.Details.Screen.Calendars(i).Description
            End If
            Me.DataWorkspace.DataSource1.SaveChanges()
        Next i
    End Sub
End Sub
```

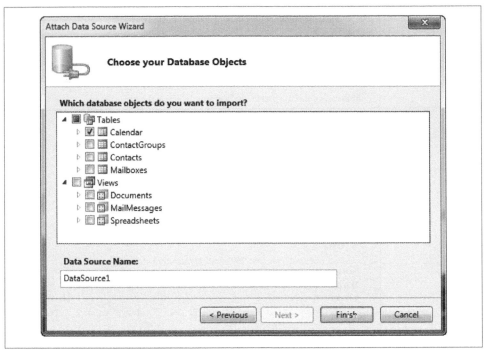

Figure 5-13. Google Data Source objects

The *for* loop is based on the number of items currently displayed on the screen. This allows you to use the built-in search tool and then send only the items returned to Google. You must provide the four fields shown in the code—StartTime, EndTime, Title, and Description—as they are required. Figure 5-14 shows what the final app looks like with only items containing "travel" displayed.

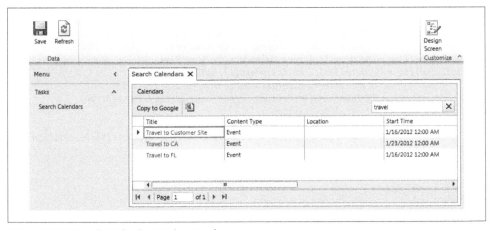

Figure 5-14. Google Calendar Update Tool

Connecting a Visual Studio LightSwitch app to any Google data sources is just that easy with the RSSBus extension. They have other extensions to connect with external data sources like Amazon SimpleDB, Facebook, Microsoft Dynamics CRM, Quick-Books, Salesforce, and Twitter (*http://www.rssbus.com/lightswitch/*).

Summary

Visual Studio LightSwitch has all the features you'll need to build first-class, stand-alone SharePoint applications. I've shown you how to use extensions for things like connecting to Google data and importing data from CSV and Excel files. I've really only scratched the surface where extensions are concerned. You can even build your own with the Microsoft extension toolkit available for download on the Visual Studio Light-Switch website.

The key takeaway here is the fact that Visual Studio LightSwitch really is a great tool for novice and experienced programmers alike. For the casual coder, it offers a way to build a custom application with little to no actual coding. It also offers a business opportunity to Independent software vendors (ISVs) looking to add value to Light-Switch through extensions. For experienced programmers, it can greatly reduce the amount of time needed to turn out quality line-of-business applications tailored to specific customer needs.

About the Author

Paul Ferrill has a BS and MS in electrical engineering and has been writing about computers for more than 25 years. He currently serves as CTO for Avionics Test and Analysis Corporation, working on multiple DoD projects. Software development has been his primary focus, along with architecting large-scale data management and storage systems. He also serves on several DoD standards committees, providing input to the next generation of data recording and transmission standards. He has a long history with both Microsoft and open source technologies. His two favorite languages are Visual Basic and Python. He's had articles published in *PC Magazine*, *PC Computing*, *InfoWorld*, *Computer World*, *Network World*, *Network Computing*, *Federal Computer Week*, *Information Week*, and multiple websites.

Get even more for your money.

Join the O'Reilly Community, and register the O'Reilly books you own. It's free, and you'll get:

- $4.99 ebook upgrade offer
- 40% upgrade offer on O'Reilly print books
- Membership discounts on books and events
- Free lifetime updates to ebooks and videos
- Multiple ebook formats, DRM FREE
- Participation in the O'Reilly community
- Newsletters
- Account management
- 100% Satisfaction Guarantee

Signing up is easy:

1. **Go to: oreilly.com/go/register**
2. **Create an O'Reilly login.**
3. **Provide your address.**
4. **Register your books.**

Note: English-language books only

To order books online:

oreilly.com/store

For questions about products or an order:

orders@oreilly.com

To sign up to get topic-specific email announcements and/or news about upcoming books, conferences, special offers, and new technologies:

elists@oreilly.com

For technical questions about book content:

booktech@oreilly.com

To submit new book proposals to our editors:

proposals@oreilly.com

O'Reilly books are available in multiple DRM-free ebook formats. For more information:

oreilly.com/ebooks

O'REILLY®

Spreading the knowledge of innovators   oreilly.com

Have it your way.

Lightning Source UK Ltd.
Milton Keynes UK
UKOW05f1053210316

270570UK00001B/67/P